THROWN OUT OF THE GARDEN

TM

For Those Who Have Eaten the Forbidden Fruit
or Would Like To

A Collection of Poetic

Thought

By

Barry Mansfield

Barry H. Mansfield

©1989–2014 U.S.A. EARTH

Order this book online at www.trafford.com
or email orders@trafford.com

Most Trafford titles are also available at major online book retailers.

Print information available on the last page.

ISBN: 978-1-4907-3210-7 (sc)
ISBN: 978-1-4907-3209-1 (e)

Library of Congress Control Number: 2021908149

Trafford rev. 02/03/2022

www.trafford.com
North America & international
toll-free: 844-688-6899 (USA & Canada)
fax: 812 355 4082

A SEED

by Barry H Mansfield

If you can plant a noble seed,

and keep it safe until it's freed

though it may trouble you indeed

no matter what the cost may be

your hour will come, hold on, true soul.

You win your prize.

You'll reach your goal

ACT

by Barry H Mansfield

You must act, not react,

never look back.

Yes, attack.

Never lack.

Attract what you want,

Rely on the font.

Live bon–viont.

Let yourself be clairvoyant.

BEAUTY

by Barry H Mansfield

Beauty, sensitivity, these are things I see
Radiating most magnificently
From the very Center of thee. Possibly if
you have, the time or inclination It would
be so fine
To sit beside you, and sip a little wine,
to entwine our fingers, most gently,
Yours in mine.
Gaze most intently into your soft warm eyes
Reflect upon the future,
About the magic waiting there
Yes, the many things your love for me could bear
If you were mine to cherish,
to comfort and to hold,
My days would not be lonely,
my nights would not be cold
If you would, sweet lady faire
Sit beside me anywhere
The sun at mourn would shine more
bright the stars more brilliant in the night.
The whole world would be just right,
If you and I were cuddled tight.

BEFORE TIME

by Barry H Mansfield

Before time, there was a space
And, in this space, there was a
face That gazed upon its face
And saw eternity in its eyes.
Alone! Just It! This
would not do!
But it knew, it knew I Just what to do!
And how and when and where it
should.
It started time within it space
And with love and grace,
it fills this space
At an ever, ever expanding pace!

It knows

It grows

It is I am!

I am It is

•

THE MAN.

The man named Jesus was a Jew
He was in fact the messiah to
He died on Golgotha for me and for you The
lord GOD resurrected him this too is true the
angles came to heal his pain
All they left was his burial cloth
With picture plain
To show he would return again!

4

BIGGER THAN YOU THINK

by Barry H Mansfield

What hurry does an immortal being have?
Something whose will alone, creates universes,
manipulates its own substance into stars
Around which grow planets
That when in just the right position
Life emerges
At first single celled
Life that has but one purpose
to live and become
Whose every mutation
Change after change after change
Strive for one thing
Contact with its source

Free will, Optimum design desired
Matter combined with energy
To create.
That which could know and love
this timeless being.
How long is the gestation period, of such life as this?
Time has no meaning, to such a being.
What is forever will forever be.

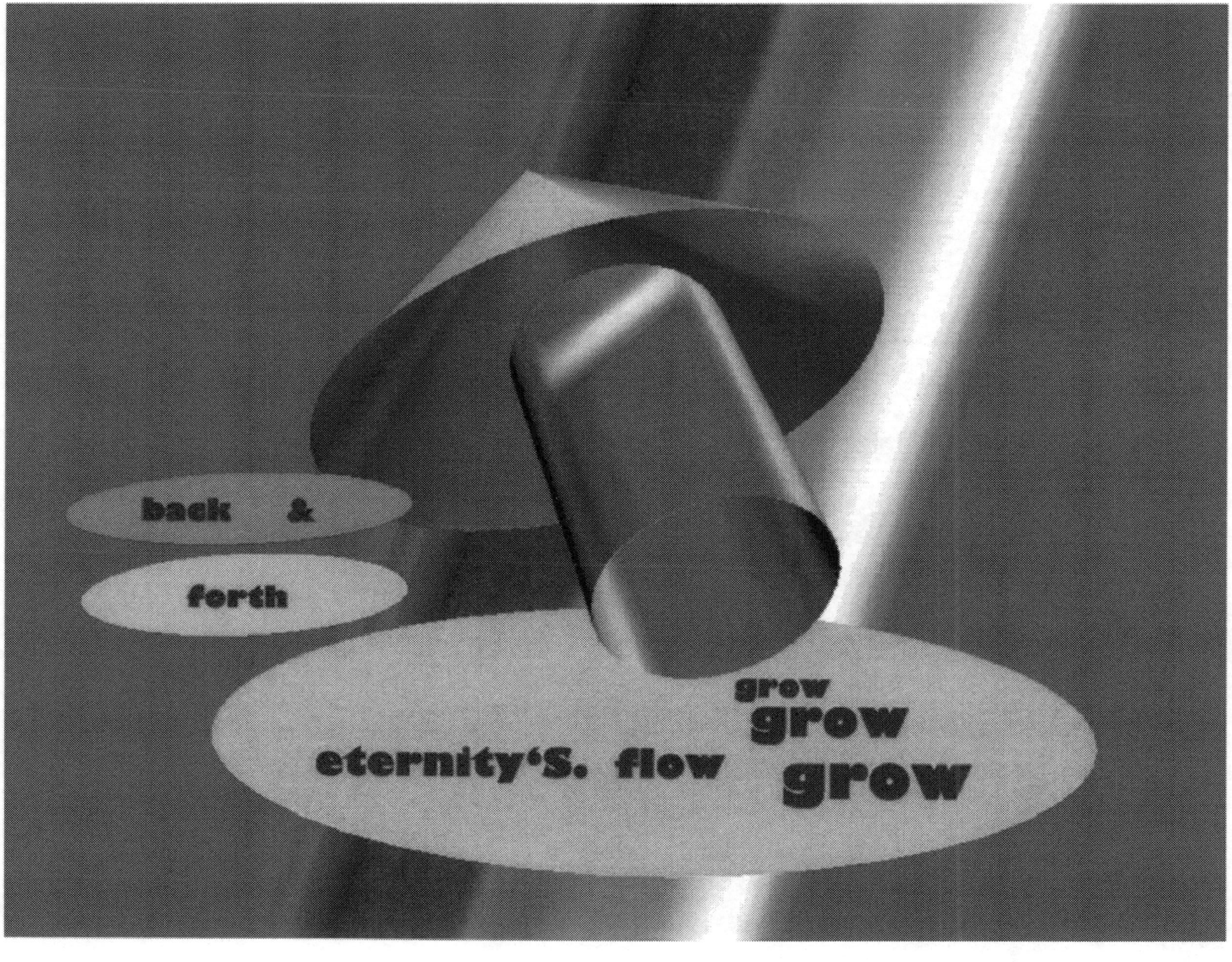
back &
forth
grow
grow
eternity'S. flow grow

BIRTH IN DEATH

by Barry H Mansfield

Vision of realities, etched upon my mind

Staring through sight-filled eyes. totally blind

Time and space have moved apart,

Not A sound no beat of heart.

Waiting for the final play,

which is just about to start?

Actors all aligned in transcendent majesty,

waiting

To receive their assigned parts in the rest of eternity.

So, you thought, this would be freedom?

Oh! You thought you would be free.

Now your mind can see forever

You know how it will be.

You can see within your soul:

You know your destiny,

there **is no place, no time in space**,

where you

will ever be free!

Unless you reassess your motives.
Understand what it is you see.
Then. maybe you will notice
You were really always free

BLESSED

by Barry H Mansfield

I look around

What do I see?

Gifts from GOD

Not gold or jewels

Yet gifts I need each day

Treasures that help

In A thousand different ways

I'm so blessed

It's hard to comprehend, God's grace

I want to return blessings received

GOD loves

They who give

As well as

Those who need

BRAVELY

by Barry H Mansfield

Through darkness

light bravely fight

Evil fear with all my might

brilliant mind yet undefined

What will it find twixt space & time

Whatever's there, all is mine

Reflections ever-changing in my mind

BUBBLE

by Barry H Mansfield

No bubble is forever So

enjoy it while it last

Explore its many colors

But you have to do it fast

For though the bubble is amazing

Pop! Before you

know it's the

past

CAN'T DO THE MATH

by Barry H Mansfield

This is written for me to see

If once more, perchance I be.

Pleasure comes in many forms.

Life causes karma.

This is something I have learned

It wasn't quick, took some time

Had to watch, look a lot

Not forget, what I have seen

Some things at first, seemed wrong to me

Then I learned, they had to be Because,

for every action

There is an equal and opposite reaction

It's so simple

The rays of the sun, make things grow

Gravity makes oceans flow

I understand the concepts

Wish I could do the math

Still, I know

I'm on the right path

And hope to relearn what I once knew.

CHANGE

by Barry H Mansfield

Paranoia! how annoying

What a bother you can be

Wish you'd go away

Truth and justice How

pleasant you can be To

bad you go away

Power through wisdom What an

experience you can be Please

don't ever go away

CHANGE!

by Barry H Mansfield

In my youth I was uncouth

But this I SAY TO YOU, for truth

To know yourself and in yourself to trust

To gain control of your emotions is a must.

CHAOS: BREAKING POINT

by Barry H Mansfield

Pressures on societies, burst the seams of reality What
is good for some, causes massive pain for others They
pay no attention to the pain that some endure
Not seeing what's in front of them
They care not--- Money-Power, their only thought,
Grief The only reality!
Violent intensity begins to shimmer in the air!
It isn't fair. It isn't fair. Why does no one care? Can't
they feel the strain that pulls upon the fabric of the lives we wear!
Disrespect, just plain nasty, who do they think they are?
Am I not flesh and blood, just as they?
I feel like they don't want me to breathe the same air, they do!
Pressure, pressure, how much can I bear?
"God" help me, this isn't right, give me a break
All I know is I'm hurting, bad, I'm mad. I'm so mad!
I don't know what to do, where to go, who to talk to,
Talk! Who the hell wants to talk! I want to do something
something bad, real, really bad.
Don't know which way to turn, or what to think.
I want this to stop, but it doesn't, stop, just gets worse,
my mind begins to unravel like a shattered piece of twine
I fall into a ravine of hate hundred meters wide,
as I melt, I flow into the streets, no longer a thinking being,
But a primal thing, caring not, moving to a savage beat,
hating everyone and everything I meet!
My head is filled with liquid fire,
Striking out at anything, rampaging, the flames grow higher,
what's this mad desire, destroy, teardown,

The flames burn higher, greed, lust, just like them
I feed the greed and desire, I am the fire.
I just don't care, I want my own, take it now,
make them bleed their liquid fire.
I see lights, here noise, means nothing, must feed desire!
Burn, burn, burn, teardown, take, I want mine, Now, Now, Now, I will get mine!
Rampaging through the streets, for hours without end.
Energy expended. I begin to feel once again, my mind starts to
real, as my senses I barely feel, numbness, recedes,
I look around, oh God! What have I done! There is
no pleasure, there is no fun, good for no one.
Mangled, wreckage, people torn and bruised
I'm so tired, want to hide, all around me disaster.
The person I am begins to feel, what I've done is more than real.
Sadness, shame is what I feel. I
pray to God for a better deal,
something kind, loving, and real.
It is my hope that one day all know
that all mankind does feel,
then learn to live and love it together.

CHILD OF LOVE

by Barry H Mansfield

IT is my mother IT is my father

I am ITs Child of love

I am nurtured & protected by IT

When the world is cruel IT comforts me

IT is a light in my night to soothe my fear

And make hope grow.

This is the reason I love IT, so.

I wish

you too could know

the treasures that I find

From something so elusive

Growing from my mind.

CLASS

by Barry H Mansfield

For my mom

I made it to the top,
I'm a success I didn't stop
Isn't it wonderful for me?
I'm so happy, I'm so free
Head of the dummy class you see

They told me I'd go far
That I'd be a real star Oh! I
made it, oh! How far, I'm so
happy, boy, that's me
I'm first class, good for me
Head of the dummy class you see

I've worked really hard, no slipshod or dull card
I'm so proud, so proud indeed
YOU too can succeed Lots of
luck, not much greed, Isn't it
great, what a deed! How I've
managed to succeed Oh boy!
Can I bleed!
Really made it, great for me!
Yes indeed,

HEAD OF THE DUMMY CLASS YOU SEE.

COALESCE

by Barry H Mansfield

To grow together

To achieve a oneness

To form a temporary or permanent union

For a goal to be reached

For an act to be complete

For a new idea to become concrete

To reach the outermost peak There

to hear GOD speak

For this oneness do I seek!

I LOVE YOU.

COMING OR GOING?

I DON'T KNOW

DO YOU?

COMPASSION

by Barry H Mansfield

Compassion is my passion

It's the only way to really be

I must live within my compassion

If I am to be truly free

If I can love all those around me

I can let all of them love me

So! I will live within my compassion

And be truly free

So, you see, Love yourself

Have compassion

It's the only way for you to really be

Yes yourself,

love yourself, have compassion

And you will Yes, you will, be truly free.

COMPLAINT

by Barry H Mansfield

What can I do, to make it through?

I'm so sad and feeling blue.

You hurt me so! You real do.

Why! Oh, why must you?

I tried to love you, yes, it's true

However, I guess in the end I only hurt you

I didn't mean to, that's for sure

Now you're gone

I miss you so

I guess it's best that you should go

DECISION'S

by Barry H Mansfield

Decision must be made
Question is, how and why
Stimulus
What we hear, see, feel, taste and touch
Never make a decision in haste
Because just maybe, it could be possible
A soul is part of a cosmic conciseness
that we are multifaceted beings
powered by a piece of this cosmic mind
And if we are, yes if we are
what is it that we must do, to help
Are kind to make it through?

What I think may not be true
What I feel may not be real
SO! How am I supposed to know?

A reassessment of my actions
An understanding of what I do & why
Will help in my quest for truth
Certainly, this is a reason for life.
SO!
Forward to eternity & truth.

TO DECIDE

by Barry H Mansfield

Simple decisions that are made

are a must

So, this ability should not

fade never, never

be afraid

of the simple decisions that have to be made

Left   Right

Off   on

Go

stop

TO BAD

by Barry H Mansfield

The fool sits in his house all day,

and disobeys the rules.

That's why you call him fool.

But what you think may not be real,

You don't care

So, from the fool you steal.

What a terrible deal,

you could care less how the fool will feel.

Listen to him squeal, what a terrible deal.

TRUTH

by Barry H Mansfield

The truth is known, the truth I speak, some
things are strange, you must not freak. If you
wish knowledge to be your own,
You must sharpen your edge,
yes, hone & hone,
Look ahead, stand alone
Will yourself!
And before GOD be known.

Movement
by Barry H Mansfield

Movement through eternity's gate
it never slows it will not wait.
No man or thing can abate this flow,
All things must, pass, all things must go.
These gates were built with purposes their own
You must eat the fruit, that's why it's grown,
Knowledge is given to those who seek
It is not for the timid, it's not for the weak

$[E=Mc2)\geq\infty$

TO TEACH AND LEARN

by Barry H Mansfield

There are many ways to reach a goal

Teach people what they need to know

Some old, some new, some tried, some true

Don't make me mad, just tell me what's true

"Take your time"

"Think it thru"

"Let it happen"

It's not more than you can do

Really want to do your best

To pass each & every test

You should know, it's up to you

To your own self

(You must be True)

You can make it, yes you can

Find the will! Have a plan!

Time & space "WILL" move apart

So step-up & do your part, don't

be ashamed of being smart

Be part of future

Succeed!

A REASON FOR CREATION

by Barry H Mansfield

The creator infuses itself into the human being to experience its own creation

feeling the joy and wonder of that creation

in all its many manifestations

what a revelation, a cause for exaltation

we carry the spark of the creator we are touched with the divine

through us it feels the sunshine

the life-giving rain

Joy happiness, sadness pain, love, and loneliness

all over and over and over again

in the multiple aspects of its own creation

renewed it each incarnation

unending in joy,

fulfillment

TODAY, TOMORROW, ETERNITY

Remembering the past today

Might help you find your norm.

TOTAL CHANGE

by Barry H Mansfield

Trust in your unused mind,
As you entrust to GOD your soul,
for it is part of the whole.

Though you may not envision the power,
that lies in this place
Its vastness is as great as outer space

Your unused mind, over gem filled troves could stroll,
look for them, but let your super ego have control, of
what appetites your heart should chase

No limit can be put on the places you may go,
Such success! No one before, has ever
gained, could be yours if you will just concede,
And GOD within your self will know.
YES, there are some who for themselves,
This prize will be attained.

WHY NOT YOU!
Move onward! SUCCEED', SUCCEED!

TRAVELING

by Barry H Mansfield

Traveling through time & space

I'm Reborn, Recreated

In a brand-new place

With a fresh face

Wonders

Now to grow —— learn

Do *my* best

Find *my* place

In the human race

WE ARE

by Barry H Mansfield

Even though suffering will not abate
and may not be pleasant or sublime
It matters not
I fight the fears and pain I find
To form the kind of fate I have in mind

We are all one people
All love one GOD
IT matters not which rites we follow
What matters is what is in our hearts
Love each other
Teach are children

Live in peace, let all prosper,
Stop the hate! Stop the war!

OPEN YOUR EYES!
OPEN YOUR EYES!
OPEN YOUR EYES!
FEEL!
FEEL!
FEEL!
LOVE!

THE TREE

by Barry H Mansfield

We are all leaves on the
tree of life
And like all leaves we die.

But have no fear, we will return.

From the tree that gives us

LIFE!

WERE I'D LIKE TO BE

by Barry H Mansfield

There is a place beyond the stars, beyond time & space
Were angels dwell, and one can gaze upon GODS face.
A place were dreams and magic have their roots Were
angle dust is not a drug, but something that falls, From
gossamer wings
Harps play music for the king of kings,
There is no dark, none sleep, nothing scary ever creeps,
through dreams which are realty.
I go there when my eyes are shut to get away from life's,
small ruts. There I find the peace of mind we all do seek
I'm not a freak; I'm loved there by one and all.
I never cry or ever fall, there is no pain or sorrow
Here there is nothing to fear,
A golden I light permeates all things
Heavenly host sing songs of peace,
Love and beauty everywhere, all around you care.

Then I awake
Face the realities of life

WHAT DO I BELIEVE

by Barry H Mansfield

IT'S HARD TO VERIFY...
THE THINGS THAT I BELIEVE:
They seem so unreal.

The thoughts I think, games I play

Cause confusion, on my way

to the life I want to grow.

Still, I think, I know, what I must do

to get to where I'm going

don't fight, just to flow

Flow right through IT

Then flow within IT

Because

IT IS what IT IS

So, flow through & in IT

WHAT & WHY

by Barry H Mansfield

What's wrong with us?

Why can't we care about each other?

What causes the fear we feel?

Why can't we teach LOVE rather than hate?

What will make us see the truth?

Why can't it happen soon?

WHATS THIS

Something calls longingly

Tenuous

My memory

Distant past

To good be cast

to joy speak

Suddenly with thee

A planer of society You

tell them were to go

Now pour suns nova

Brightly

Turn v ital. novae stars

Producing civilization, people

See destiny triumph

Smoldering, volatile

Static ceases tomorrow

GODS just biology

WHY

by Barry H Mansfield

Coming and going, going, or coming

Don't remember why or what

What *do* I know?

All that I was

What I am, what I can be,

Ignorance of the world

My ignorance

Which is worse?

Both bad

Can't stand it, causes me pain

Must keep moving forward

Look ahead, choose my path

Move onward to where I want to be

Do what I think is right

Remember

WHY

I'm coming and

going

I DON'T GET IT

by Barry H Mansfield

What possible fury, could hold such weight,
To stop my query at such a late date.
Be I fool or king what possible thing
Could cause a reply
That would be somewhat nicer
Then, I spit in the eye.

GIVE

Give to someone, give today
To someone, some love
and tomorrow will come
A gift from above.

START

The time has come at last to start on a new path

That moves into the future, but not to, fast

The nature of existence makes it practical to move slow

while keeping a steady motion, the way most things grow

Time moves on, stars circle in their path

Always moving forward never looking back.

When people are pushed faster than they can grow

It only causes confusion, this all should know

So, move along your path, with a pace steady and strong

You'll get to where you're going, it won't take too long.

WIN OR LOSE

by Barry H Mansfield

You can win or you can lose

It will be just as you choose

To be a fool or be a king

Either way it's the real thing

So, when you pick which way it will be.

Be sure to open your eyes, so you can see.

YOU AND ME

by Barry H Mansfield

I by myself am nobody,
But when I'm with you I'm somebody
With you by my side theirs harmony
Without you all I feel is discord

ALONE

by Barry H Mansfield

She sits in the sand by the sea without me.
I stand in the sand by the sea without she.
I'd like you to bring her to me
WOULD YOU PLEASE?

WINTER'S GONE

by Barry H Mansfield

Winter's gone; at last warm air,

The breezes so gentle, so sweet and fair

Our hearts are at ease

The flowers so pretty, blow in the soft breezes

Beauty all around us, love that pleases

standing in the midst of you

Your fragrant scent,

Overpowering, lingers on

reminders of soft spring

Gentle touching, feeling,

Stand still, sway

Your memory forever on the shores of my mind.

YESTERDAY GONE

by Barry H Mansfield

Yesterday's gone it was only a dream of the
past there is only remembrance, Tomorrows
a vision thrown on hopes screen A will-o-
the-wisp a mere semblance
Why morn & grieve over yesterday's ills
Or paint memories pictures with sorrows
Why worry or fret for worrying kills Over
things that won't happen tomorrow
Yesterday gone it shall never return
Peace to its ashes and calm
Tomorrow no human has ever discerned
Still hope, trust, and faith are its balm This
moment is all that I have of my own to
use well or waste as I may
For I know that my future depends alone
On the things that I do today
This moment my past and my future I form
I can make it want ever I choose
By the deeds & the acts I now perform
By the words and the thoughts that I use So
I fear not the future nor morn for the past
Cause I do all I'm able today
Living each moment as through it were
My last
Perhaps it is, who knows,
Who can say?

YOU OR ME

by Barry H Mansfield

What am I to you or me?
The difference is in the way we see
If I, were you, and you looked at me,
I could tell at a glance; you want to be free
So, when you look at me just see me as thee.

WHEN

by Barry H Mansfield

When you mind your own business
And do it well
It's one step out of the grave
And one away from hell

When you think about tomorrow
As well as yesterday
And take care of responsibilities
EACH and EVERY day

You will find that life is good
In the most amazing ways
Heaven cannot be far
Love is a true sound
Within its resonance
Peace can be found

YOU SAY

by Barry H Mansfield

You say you can't love me,

For I have no riches,

I say if you'd love me,

I'd even dig ditches,

For love is the greatest wealth, man's ever known

Look through the ages it's clearly shown

YOU THINK

by Barry H Mansfield

People think, there so righteous,

They know it all.

The truth is, they don't, know,

At all.

They feel, what they think,

Everyone should.

Well, that would be fine,

If they were truly good.

But there're, NOT.

To, bad for us!

They have the power

I'm happy for them

Share it with me

I like it too!

DOES THIS MAKE SENSE

by Barry H Mansfield

Put evil from my life
Orient my sensibilities

Please christen my ideas
Divest me of my troubles
Add kindness to my list of doings
Protect me from jealousy
I strive most of the time, because
special thought is rarely lost

To days ideas die hard, new
visions are not for sure
Sadness is not wise to bring

Free me from drudgery
and see stars shine
Nova my potential

Sadness precedes nothing but junk
Positive thought improves your risk

DIRECTION

by Barry H Mansfield

Reaching for the devil or reaching for God

Takes the same amount of effort.

When one asks for power, at that point,

they, have a choice

to use it ill or good

to have sorrow or rejoice

both these paths are open to

move you must choose one

I wish good luck to you

I hope you will have fun

DIRECTION FOR

Unproductive creative intelligence
Will cause trouble in society
If not directed into proper channels!

HOW, WHAT & WHY

With all the energy we can find with

all the information in our minds

Because we want the human race

TO SURVIVE!

DISGRAPHIA

by Barry H Mansfield

Words, numbers in sequence flow

I try so hard; I want to know, these things,

Lost, within the recesses of my mind,

Almost, impossible to find

when I was young, this caused me pain

I trained my brain with much hard work

To disassociate, not to strain, so I may go

To what I want to find, Buried in the discord

Within the pathways of my mind

DON'T KNOW

by Barry H Mansfield

Don't know what to do
Or how to handle it

Get an idea in your head
Don't want it'
Won't leave
Just can't get rid of it

It's not beneficial
It's doesn't make you happy

Still draws you
Moth to flame

Results the same
What a shame

EXTRA! EXTRA!

See it happen

DREAMS

by Barry H Mansfield

Dreams can be a fleeting thing
Or last a thousand years
Cause fear, or bring lost love quite near
Real or unreal, possibility of the impossible
Forever in your mind
Worlds within worlds can you find
Not realty but they keep you sane ease the pain
Something else will do the same
Think about someone else, ease their pain
So much to gain it may not be easy
Still, think about someone else anyway
You may find yourself.
They need you; you need them.
Change one thing, all life changes
Good or bad, it's up to you
It all becomes new, help where you can
Nothings safe, nothings clear, face your fear
Your vision will come to you
You may find peace, it's worth the chance
See all the beauty that can be
It's all for you and it's free

ENOUGH

by Barry H Mansfield

Prices rise & rise & rise, rise & rise

Come on people open your eyes

More, more, more, more & more

Give more don't take more

Want less, give more

When your vessel's full, quit filling

Be content

Thank that, from which all things flow.

Time flows, all things change

in this life

we are all part of time.

Go with the flow

be flexible not rigid.

Let things find their level.

Don't worry, be happy.

EXPECTATION

by Barry H Mansfield

I wake with good expectation

I wish I could,

I think I can,

I have a plan

GOD knows

I'm only man

FAITH PRECEEDS
THE MIRACLE

by Barry H Mansfield

If you are to succeed, you must believe

No act or deed, should go unnoticed

Step out of the tunnel in which you've been liven'

No doubt you'll be forgiven

Let lightness turn off the dark

Intuition be the spark who's Flames

rise in the sky

meet them with open eyes

Peace & beauty shall be your prize

Keep on liven, we have been forgiven

They grow you know

FOR WHOM OR WHAT

by Barry H Mansfield

LIFE, LIBERTY AND THE PURSUIT OF HAPPINESS

These are the words our founding fathers used,
To express their desire for individual freedom.

What do these words mean?
Do they have any meaning?

Can we the people of the twenty-first century
Relate to these words?
Yes, we can,
But how?

Which is more important, a person or bombs?
What should come first, love or money?

What is more important?
Children, education, health and nation or war

Welfare of state, Welfare of people,
Frame of reference, ship of state,
Relative concepts, state no absolute motion
The measurement of nonmaterial substance

HUMAN FORMULA= RESPONSIBILITY

FORMATION

by Barry H Mansfield

Time, moves through unformed space

As it moves, it forms

The days we see

Ever changing norms

Realities, both good and bad

Are formed, by and from this flow

Time, an interdependent thing

Is here to help things grow

FREEDOM

by Barry H Mansfield

War is an unpleasant affair
How much is freedom worth? Ask
a minuteman, a union soldier
Talk to those who lie in Flanders fields
Don't like war
Despise it
YET
I will pay the price
When Europe fell & London burned
Isolation was our thought
We didn't want to get involved
Bombs fell on Hawaii's shore
Had no choice
For freedom we said

Don't like war
Despise it
Still, I will pay the price
Freedom from what or whom
the question has to be asked

I ask that question "What price freedom?"

Don't like war
Despise it
No matter I will pay the price
And ask the question,
why

FROM IT TO US

by Barry H Mansfield

To Moses GOD said these things

I have brought you out of bondage
I ask this of you

You shall have no other GOD
I am the infinite a form that can be seen,
therefore,
you shall not make any image or any likeness
Of anything that is in the heavens, or on the earth, or under it
Love me and my creation, keep my commandments
I will love you and all your generation

Take time to remember me and my creation
Honor your mother and father
Do not kill
Do not commit adultery
Do not steal
Do not lie about anybody
Do not want other people's things

Moses asked, what, is your name

GOD said

IT IS I AM
I AM IT IS

HEAD TO HEART

by Barry H Mansfield

You blow my mind,
Your actions undefined,
Slow down, and love you'll find

OH! It's great to lust and fuck
But without LOVE, IT'LL BRING BAD
LUCK!

Love me slow; give our love a chance to grow,
I want you now I want you so, But Slow,
No hurry in passions haste
The years of love for us to waste

Lust and passion you can find
Greed and jealousy will blow your mind, it's
hard in this world when you want to be kind.

HAIKU'S & IF

by Barry H Mansfield

A TIME TO TALK
It past so fast
Will it come again?

A smile a sigh
I could have stayed forever
Too bad I left

BOOM, BOOM, BOOM! She
touched my hand, my cheek and
now she's gone

IF

If you want me to love you
Like you want to be loved
Just think of me and GOD above
I will love you to the end of time.
I will be yours, you will mine
Our love will be so fine

I PRETEND

by Barry H Mansfield

I pretend that someone loves me
I pretend that someone cares Yet
I'm sinking in an ocean, There's
really no one there

I'm falling through the air
There's no one there

I WANT SOMEONE TO CARE

I'm sinking in quicksand
No one's there

Is there

I've fallen many times
Never hit the bottom
‘’’’……’,,,,’\,,,,,,,,,,,,,,,,,,,,,,,’,,,,’’’’’’’,,,,,,,’’
IS SOMEONE THERE

I AM WORLD

by Barry H Mansfield

I am a world, communication allows me

To visit other worlds

Well not so much visit as exchange ideas

Try to get a perspective on other worlds

See how well they fit my own

Sometimes I even get lucky and learn

A little about another world

This makes me want to get closer to that world

Or run as fast as I can

Cosmic pool, don't be a fool

Pay attention, that's the rule

You only get out as much as you put in

Have fun learn

I BELIEVE THAT

by Barry H Mansfield

I believe trying to do something
Is better than not doing anything
Self-indulgence is fine
If you don't want to get anywhere

Free will is a given
That makes the choice up to us
Harmony or discord what shall it be
Slavery, freedom, it's up to me
Excuses; excuses; their more than enough

Oh! Poor me, I can't do this
Oh! Poor me; I can't do that

Think as little of yourself as you want
You want to be afraid, be afraid
Want to be a coward, so be it

You want to be blessed
Stop putting yourself down
Do! what you can't
Don't cry and moan, about what you think is

Create a miracle, believe you can

Yes! Free will is a given!

I
AM

by Barry H Mansfield

=I am not a sheep
To be led

I am a light shining
On blind eyes

I am a voice shouting
To deaf ears

I am knowledge trying to be spread
To the ignorance that permeates
Itself through the ages

I AM HOPE!

I
BELIEVE
And
It's OK

by Barry H Mansfield

The changing
winds
of
time
&
space
they
form
the
Human
race.

There is no place,
there is no space,
that is not
filled with GOD.
So have no fear,
for it is near,
and never ever far.

IT'S OK
I know that you don't believe what I believe,
and that's all-right.
Still, I believe what I believe,
and that's OK!

I DO BUT I DON'T

by Barry H Mansfield

You tell me, change this, and change that,
OK:
I hear you, I know your trying
To help.
I don't doubt your ability,
Or your expertise
But you ask me to be someone I'm not!

True, I'd like to please you,
Be accepted, you know,
What cost, to me?
Don't want to be you,
Just want to be
Want to be me!

I may never be accepted,
So maybe that's the price I have to pay

Truth is I don't know what to do.
I'm ambivalent
Too comfortable in my fantasies of grandeur.

Realty always disappoints me.
Just want to love & be loved!

I SEE YESTERDAY

by Barry H Mansfield

I see yesterday, followed

By tomorrow through today,
but I don't have a thing to say!

About tomorrow or yesterday.

But I can tell you about today.

I watch as you fall
you fall as I watch
I fall with you
We are alone together
with everything else

Good or bad don't be sad

It's bound to changes soon

I'M NOT

By Barry H Mansfield

I'm not suffering from badness
But from lack of goodness

Don't take, with selfish greed
Do what's right and lead

All should become leaders
People feeders

IN MY TIME

By Barry H Mansfield

I have everything, I have nothing
I am a sinner, I am a saint
I am what I and the world have made me
Who and what this really is, I hope someday to know -
-If I have enough time to find out

My body exists for just a single second
In time
Although, I may exists through-out eternity

Love has been found and lost
I have destroyed myself in many ways
I have hope, which lies in my quest for future
knowledge

Don't seem to have what people want
Just might have something they need

Life cuts hard, makes you bleed
Takes more than luck to succeed
the blessings I receive, they come
From human love and compassions seed

I march through time my head held high
KNOWING
That all I can do is try!

IS WHAT IS

by Barry H Mansfield

If it is to be

It's up to me

Therefore

I will be better and

better every day

Better and better in

every way!

IT COULD BE WORSE

by Barry H Mansfield

This sadness is *beyond*, Beyond
My being overcome
Waves of unexplained misery
Somethings I know, I don't want to know
Do I have time to learn & grow?
Some things I may never known
Unfortunate!

Though
I do know that even though
I'm overwhelmed sometimes
With
Sensations of pain & anguish
Life could be worse

THERE IS STILL HOPE!

IT'S UP TO YOU

From the twelve golden power books

There is no chance, no circumstance no fate

That can circumvent nor hinder nor control

the firm resolve of a determined soul

Gifts count for nothing will alone is great

All things give way before it soon or late

What obstacle can stay the mighty force

of a sea seeking river in its course

Or cause the never-ending orb of day to wait

Each well-born soul must win what it deserves

Let the fools talk of luck

The fortunate are they whose Ernest purpose never swerves

Whose slightest action or inaction serves the one great aim

Why even death itself stands still,

And waits, an hour sometimes,

For such a will

LET IT BE

by Barry H Mansfield

The history of are race has been

An insane bloody disgrace

In order to justify it, we revere

murder of a great man

What a pity, what a shame.

God or man, right or wrong

Who cares theirs only been one

All along,

were all part of it,

can't you see.

hear my words

Let it be, peace and justice, let it be!

LIFE IS

by Barry H Mansfield

Life is strange, strange, strange.
So very hard to arrange, arrange
How much of it actually out of your range
To recreate or rearrange?

If you think life's flow is hard to move
about, You're Right!
But! Don't give up or get uptight!
Stand up straight!
Begin to fight! Will things right,
With all your might!
It's your right! It is your right.
Think of yourself as a shining knight
Fight for your right!

But keep it light, 'is better for the sight
And you will find though it is strange
There is a way to rearrange
Nothing is really out of your range
You can change or recreate
All those things which we call fate.

It's not too late!
Don't hesitate, or procrastinate,
why wait,
Time will not abate,
It is your F.A.T.E.
(Excelcyate)
DON'T WAIT
You'll get things straight, It's
really...Really, not too late,
It may be strange, strange, strange
But you can DO IT!

GO AHEAD!

LIVE OR SLOWLY DIE

by Barry H Mansfield

Loneliness is a chronic pain
Hard to stand, harder to explain

Caught in a cold hard rain

Minutes like hours, never ending days
Self-incriminations, what a shame
The longer it lasts, the more intense the strain
Loss of everything we have ever loved Thinking
you're responsible, hoping you're not

Not much is for sure-- So

Think less about the past
Dwell upon the future's hope
Do something positive

Don't sit around and mope
Handle the pain
find a way

Out of the rain

LIVED

by Barry H Mansfield

I've lived through forever,

It was only, yesterday

I've lived through forever

now I live for today

Your hand in mine

Feels so fine

Warmth of a new day I

love through forever

Please stay...It'll be ok

LONGTIME

by Barry H Mansfield

It's been so long since I've had peace of mind.

It's been so long since I've had self-respect.

I know not where or how to find these things,

My mind still bright, yet dimmed by pain,

Surges still, through mist and rain

A sad song, mournful refrain, time is lost

I cannot explain I only know I can't maintain

The fantasies through which I've lived

I want them; to die!

I want to live!

I have much, much, more to give

LOTS OF LOVE

by Barry H Mansfield

Things could get better, and they just might

if we can start caring more about each other

and less about who's wrong or right.

The past which was our yesterday

has seen us yell and fight.

try to hurt each other, with all our might.

What a waste of strength that was

and what a waste of time.

So, let's think about tomorrow or even just today.

I wish only to love and live-in harmony.

It is for peace I pray!

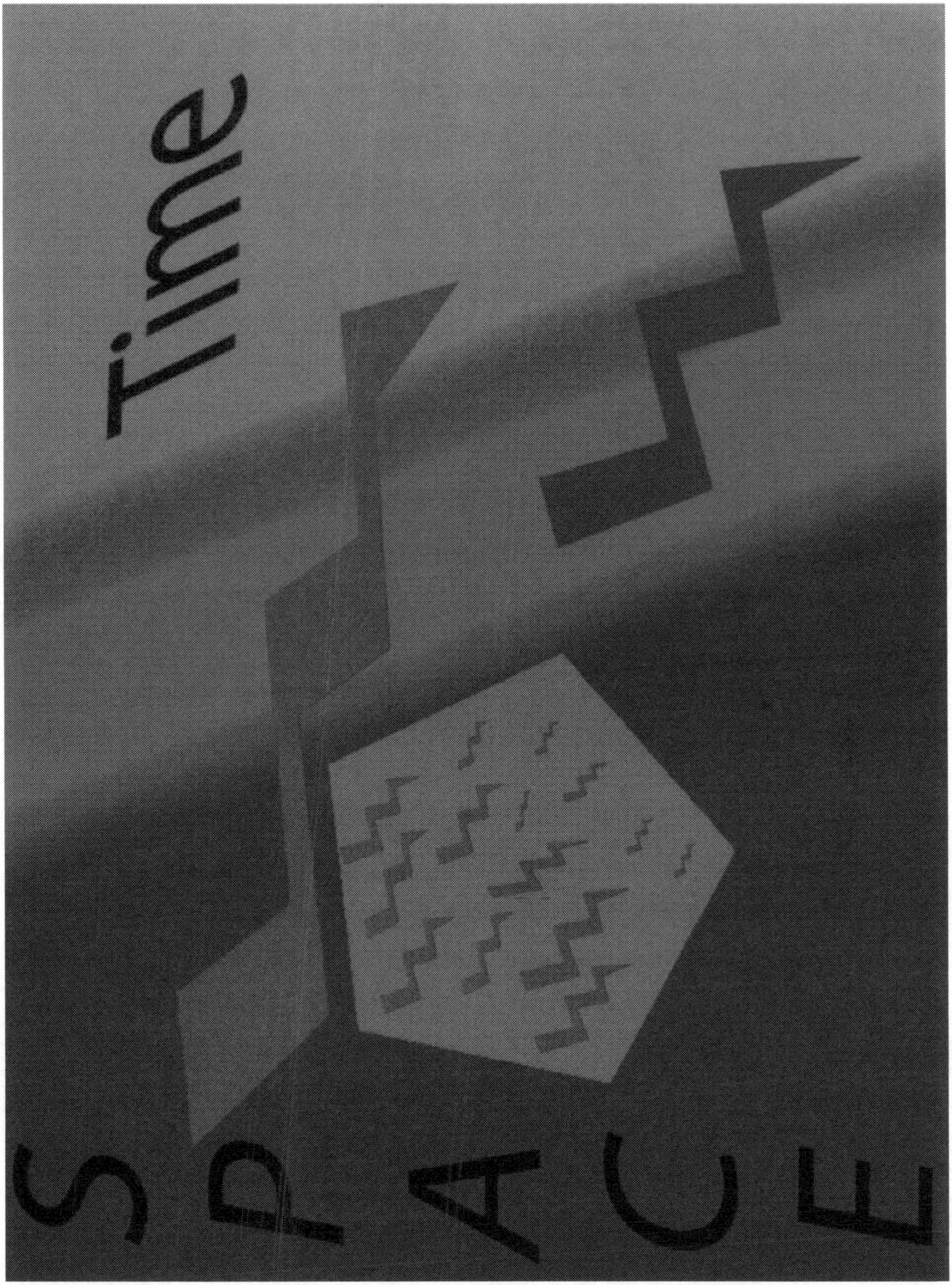
Time
SPACE

LOVE SHOULD

by Barry H Mansfield

Love must not be taken

Lightly

Love should be shown, let shine

brightly

Love should be shared, both day &

nightly

Love should care, yes! Care most

rightly

Love should be held, both gently &

tightly

LOVES RIDE

by Barry H Mansfield

Passions ride on love's tide

they slide and glide

sigh and cry

lie and die, tried,

they subside

abide and divide

this division sustains their optimum duration

[To wit, effectiveness.)

MAGIC

by Barry H Mansfield

My first poem

What magic in the darkness

Among the treasures in one's mind

What fortunes and what blessings can one find?

Of the power and enlightenment that here too in do dwell

Can we find our true fulfillment

and escape this earthbound

Hell

MAKE SENSE OF THIS

by Barry H Mansfield

Put evil from my life
Orient my sensibilities

Please christen my ideas
Divest me of my troubles
Add kindness to my list of doings
Protect me from jealousy
I survive most of the time,
Because special thought is rarely lost

To days ideas die hard new
visions are not for sure
Sadness is not wise to bring

Free me from drudgery
and sec stars shine
Nova my potential

Sadness precedes nothing but junk
Positive thought improves your risk
Something calls longingly
Tenuous

My memory
Distant past
To good be cast
To joy speak

Suddenly with thee
A planer of society
You tell them were to go
Now pour suns nova

Brightly

Tum vital novae stars
producing civilization, people
See destiny triumph
Smoldering. volatile
Static ceases tomorrow
GODS just biology

MAYBE I DO

by Barry H Mansfield

At this space in time

We only have one world

It's green & blue, full of life

A blessing on us all

Yet I, sit alone and wait

While I and the world

change Why I'm waiting I'm

not sure

I cry & cry about what is not now

Then I start again

In and on this being where we do

dwell

Are all things possible?

I think, yet I don't know

When I was a child, I wanted to know so much

Now I'm grown, I still do.

MAYBE I WAS AND EFFORT

by Barry H Mansfield

Maybe I was he who sat on a high dais
Watched those he thought belonged to him
Or the one who wrote upon the wall
I know it, I know it, it's going to blow
Maybe the one who created poems
Which are the keys to real power
Yet never singed their name
So, what!
Nothing exists except this moment
What I do this second is all that counts
How I deal with the pressure & pain of daily life
Will decide how the next second shall be
It's really not hard to comprehend the
realty is I'm only a human being
There's no maybe, I'm me

EFFORT
To reach the devil or to reach God
takes the same amount of effort.
When one asks for power, at that point,
they have a choice.
to use it for ill or good, to
have sorrow or rejoice,
both these paths are open.
To move you must choose one.
I wish good luck to you.
I hope you will have fun.

MEANDER

by Barry H Mansfield

To meander down the lane of life

All filled with care and woe and strife

Is a very useless thing to do.

You should not cry and mope or feel blue

For blue is the color of the sky

When the sun is out, and earth and air are dry

Your soul should fly and dream of loves repast

GET ON WITH LIVING, YES! HAVE A BLAST

NEST

by Barry H Mansfield

Love is a two-way street

a little nest where we can sleep

and feel our toes feet to feet

a quiet place for us to meet

NEVER

by Barry H Mansfield

Never watch the words, yet!

Always watch the person

Who says them!

ODE TO A YOUNG GODDES

by Barry H Mansfield

You are a vision divine
Ruby lips on mine, nectar, sweet wine
Golden hair, sunshine through air
Eyes shine like stars, diamond bright,
Every aspect just right

Love me forever, be my lady fair
Let me love, give me a chance to care

Sweet moments in eternity, silver bells that chime
Ecstasy could be ours if you were mine Diana,
virgin goddess of the hunt
Moon goddess; shine on me your silver light
That I may see to fight the loneliness,
which clouds my night.
Give me the love you hold tight,
A blessing saved for a wondrous night.
Visions of love, I see with you,
Goddess of love,

My love is true!

PART SAINT, PART SINNER

Both LOOSE

Neither's a Winner!

PETITE LADY

by Barry H Mansfield

Petite Lady with eyes silver blue

I'd like to get closer to you

I imagine the warmth of your touch,

You loving me would mean so much

Gentle Lady with eyes silver, blue,

Warm inviting smile, kind sweet voice,

When your eyes turn toward me

and you say hello,

I light up inside with a special glow,

And

though time & space may separate us

I want you to know that as time moves,

My love will grow,

PLEASE

by Barry H Mansfield

Please dear GOD, hear my plea,
Help make life right for me
Show me how to correct my faults
Open to me your storage vaults and
from your stores, of vast supplies
Send fourth to me the knowledge
On which I can rely
To make my life productive and full

I know somewhere in time & space,
There is a special place
where I can have peace of
mind,
be both generous & kind,
Not continuously driven out of my mind,
by what is right or what is wrong,
were, I can sing my own true song
All around me love will dwell.

Please dear GOD
Just one chime,
From your bell, so I will know
So, I can tell, that all the time's, that I fell
Had a purpose,
I beg this, with all my might!
Let me find my place, and make things right

PRECIOUS

by Barry H Mansfield

A beast they are not

Although they look like

Humans are not they

Unicorns are to me

Gods most precious being

YET

Humans are to be most of all

That I can see!

QUESTING SELF

by Barry H Mansfield

The eagle flies through turquoise skies

Above the painted plain

Proud, strong, without fear

Master of its domain

Through blowing winds, brilliant sun

Sometimes–mighty rains

The beauty of its awesome flight

Symbol of A great idea

May its quest be long and far

The eagle flies for you & me

Be free

REALITY

by Barry H Mansfield

THE WAY I THINK,
Controls my life
It cuts much deeper than a surgeon's knife
Love is so real
You can taste and touch steel,
So, you know what you feel
YES, life too is real
My heart surely beats
My pulse often quickens
As I run through the nights
Fears sometimes beckon
Yet! I keep moving on
For I know what I am
A creature of GOD who is spawned from man
Time never stops
Nor shall it ever return
So, I look ahead
And I watch and I yearn
And with love and compassion,
I see myself grow
And though time move on

I KNOW THAT I KNOW!

REFLECTIONS

by Barry H Mansfield

Reflections of forgotten things, cast upon my mind.

Waiting there for me, one day to find.

Things I knew and things I know.

How to be, which way to go

As I catch their glimmerings,

they help me live and make me grow.

RELATIVE EXPERIENCE

by Barry H Mansfield

Life is an experience in relativity

Hours sometimes slow

Sometimes fast

Days crawl by or fly

Years go by in a single breath

Relatively, so do I

I often wonder why

No matter what the pace may be

Something stays the same

I don't know what IT is

Can't quite give IT a name

but listen

Do you hear IT?

EXPERIENCE AND

by Barry H Mansfield

Obsessed by a memory, it happens to us all

Causes a stop, a dysfunctional stall

Growth is stopped, energy is plugged yet,

Transcendental knowledge a reflection of a shadow,

Captured by a mind, presses upon your conciseness

Impossible to define,

all that can be learned may not be enough,

to understand this shadow,

this reflection of a thought.

All the years that I have lived, abide within me still

and talk to me in distant plaintiff call

as the many years seek to be relived

I quest into the future, searching for the light

through loneliness surrounds me like a fog turned into ice

I persevere

REMEMBER

by Barry H Mansfield

When you lose someone, you love a lot

Remember

That's not all you've got

So, look through things that you have left

See what you find

Try to

Keep the good things

In the forefront of your mind

REPRESSION

by Barry H Mansfield

Do you believe in an immortal soul?

How about energy,

Or matter?

Does this make a difference?

Yes! I think, it does

WHY? This

is why:

Matter can be turned into energy,

Energy can change to matter

These are the only two states

That exists.

Your body is matter & energy

Matter can decay

What happens to the energy?

I don't know,

do you?

I believe energy goes somewhere.

What do you think?

I don't know, for sure

Still, I think.

RULES

by Barry H Mansfield

Rules and regulations which everyone must know

They don't do much for you

They don't help you grow

You say, I must Listen,

That they're good for me.

I tell you they're not, I want to be free!

I see your well meaning

But you, you can't see,

The ten that God gave us, Are good enough for me.

I respect your right to live your own life.

So, stop cutting me down, with your dull edge knife!

I to want to live my own life,

So let me be!

I say that I will!

(YES, I MUST BE FREE!!!)

SOMETHINGS

by Barry H Mansfield

Some things I can get

Myself, to do

Some things I have An

aversion to.

STRANGE PLACE

by Barry H Mansfield

In a strange place
Caught between worlds

Torn twisted Lies
Misdirection
Fire burns
Ice-contractions

The mind seethes
Body shuts off

Up becomes down
Down--up
Reversal revision
Clarity indecision

Life follows death
Possible redemption
in a strange place

THE GIFT

by Barry H Mansfield

In the beginning was the word

Then the word became manifest in man

Yet man did not understand the word

Still the word gave man dominion over earth

Yet man was like a child, grown, without knowledge

So, the word reached into the minds of the few, who

felt more deeply.

Those few began to understand the word

Causing the light of the word to shine **in** them

So that they could teach the meaning of,

The word to all men.

THE WINDS OF CHANGE

by Barry H Mansfield

In the land before time

It was so fine

Life itself was sublime

Everything in its own time

Instant gratification

Changed the scene

Electric fire real mean

Wait for nothing, want it now!

Doesn't matter, who or how

All thoughts about lust and greed

Try to find someone you can trust

What a world, makes me sad

Doesn't have to be, so bad

I believe there's

hope

Cause: people are born & will be born

The future they shall make

I pray they have the will and sight to see

The winds of change blow constantly

THINGS COME IN WAVES

by Barry H Mansfield

Inspiration   Desperation

Manic pleasure----manic pain

Brilliant sunshine, torrent rain

Nothing simple, quite insane

Memories the vehicle of hope

Hope relieves the strain

With this we can remember and learn

To be whom that we want to be

without struggle we are doomed to self-indulgence

It's not simple; still, it's worth the time

Time of which there is so little

Within which we have so much to gain

Remember the past
Look to the future
Live the minute

It is the way, to a better day

THINKING

by Barry H Mansfield

I can say, "I think; therefore, I am"

Though what I think, may not be

Still, I'm really sure I'm me,

true there is a chance, it's not true

But it's almost sure, I'm not you

Thinking, about this makes me blue

You know what, that's not true

cause if I was blue, I wouldn't be.

ME

HUMANISTIC APPROACH

by Barry H Mansfield

Inspired by Philosophers, Charles Mills and Mark Rockwell

Intersectionality the many-sided key

shaped by oppression and privilege

must somehow fit the lock, that will! Set mankind free!

Personal Response Association, a thought to forge the key

An understanding of the hierarchy of privilege and oppression

a mighty task, a humongous deed,

there is no way around it. There's nothing else to do.

A dealing with reality, that must be addressed,

a change in understanding, a readjustment of the self,

throughout all society, to the very depths of our being.

A true comprehension, and justice as never known before,

waits with celestial understanding, behind this massive door.

This lock, this door, and key,

will be formed from every discipline

within humanity.

IN COMMON

by Barry H Mansfield

It's true, we are different, in many ways

Still

we all get hungry! And need a breath of air

and

water is quite essential to our good health

but

we can give thanks, that we all don't think the same

considering

that if we did our lives would sure be boring

essentially

were copied from a master form

though

differences do appear, making us different

possibly

our need for love, consideration of, and

respect

can

make us see each other, as we would be seen.

UNIVERSAL FORMS

by Barry H Mansfield

What is truth? What is justice? What is honor?

What are the forms that are not norms?

They are a universal design,

that exist within humanity soul

they are real, it is possible to understand them

by allowing all to becoming a universal whole. Socrates

and Plato were among the first to tell us so, the

question is, how is it that such as man should know? It

was only an idea, a concept, a formulating thought and

here is where the idea of forms does start

within the mind of man with time to think

of things that might be and how they might become.

UNIVERSAL MULTIPLICITY

Or something I believe Mite be

by Barry H Mansfield

Master, miracle, mystery

Grand design

change of tune, too small to see

multiple vibrations

of infinity

to

multiple universes

the woven strands of universal desire

all we know, and all we don't

ever-changing Symphony of realities

light and matter seem to be the same

could this possibly be end game